How to Make a Folding Machine for Sheet Metal Work

Designed and written by Rob Hitchings

Step-by-step instructions on how to build a versatile machine for folding sheet metal to produce box sections e.g. ducting and pans/trays etc. Includes detailed plans, operating instructions, and several design options.

Practical
ACTION
PUBLISHING

Intermediate Technology Publications 1985

Practical Action Publishing Ltd 27a
Albert Street, Rugby,
CV21 2SG, Warwickshire, UK
www.practicalactionpublishing.org

© Intermediate Technology Publications 1987.

First published 1987\Digitised 2013

ISBN 10: 0 90303 176 0
ISBN 13: 9780903031769
ISBN Library Ebook: 9781780442358
Book DOI: http://dx.doi.org/10.3362/9781780442358

Since 1974, Practical Action Publishing (formerly Intermediate Technology Publications and ITDG Publishing) has published and disseminated books and information in support of international development work throughout the world. Practical Action Publishing is a trading name of Practical Action Publishing Ltd (Company Reg. No. 1159018), the wholly owned publishing company of Practical Action. Practical Action Publishing trades only in support of its parent charity objectives and any profits are covenanted back to Practical Action (Charity Reg. No. 247257, Group VAT Registration No. 880 9924 76).

Acknowledgements

Financial assistance in the final development of this machine as well as in the production of this booklet was made available through Intermediate Technology Industrial Services from a grant from the Overseas Development Administration. Their assistance is gratefully acknowledged.

Acknowledgement is also given to Rob Hitchings' colleagues at ApT Design and Development, Blockley, Gloucestershire, who assisted in the production of this manual.

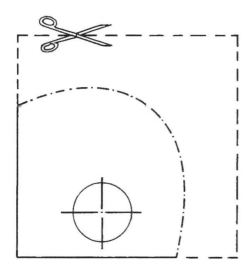

Pattern for cam
refer to page 24

Cut out square.
Tape on to metal.
Centre punch through
pattern on dots and
pivot centre.

Introduction

The sheet metal folding machine, the construction of which is described in detail in this booklet, is cheap to build and versatile in use. It can be made from readily-available channel, angle and hollow steel sections using basic welding and fabrication techniques. The only equipment essential to its construction is a drilling machine, an electric welder, G clamps and basic hand tools. An angle grinder, mechanical hacksaw and a flame cutter would make it easier, though these tools are not essential.

Construction can be modified to suit locally-available materials. The machine can be bolted on to a strong bench or mounted on a stand.

Once constructed, this machine will be found very useful in any small metal workshop to make objects in sheet metal such as boxes, trays, baking-pans, channels, air-ducts, chimney flues, funnels, cabinets; or agricultural equipment such as seed-hoppers, troughs, water and fuel tanks.

This folding machine should prove an invaluable tool in any small workshop in the industrialized countries, as well as in the Third World.

Important Notice to Constructors

★   The plans and instructions given in this manual **must** be read very carefully **at each step** of the construction process.
★   The order described here in which parts are made and assembled is the easiest, and should be followed exactly.
★   Particular care must be given to the relative positions of parts before they are welded.
★   Where materials are not available in the sizes specified in the manual, give serious thought as to how your substitution with material of a different size will affect the function of that part of the machine:
    — Will the change weaken the finished machine?
    — Will it make the machine less durable?
    — Will this substitution alter other dimensions given elsewhere in the manual?
★   Where flat bar or plate of the specified thickness is not available, consider whether you could weld two thinner pieces together around the edges and use this in its place.
★   It is usually better to use a larger steel section than a smaller one.
★   Components which slide together or rotate in one another should not be painted on those surfaces, and should be greased or oiled as the machine is assembled. Further oiling from time to time will also prolong the life of the machine.
★   At the back of this manual is a check list. Please read it both before you build the machine and after you have completed the machine. If all the points listed are OK you will be well pleased with your machine!

Contents

4

Manufacturing and testing the machine in Botswana.

Uses of the folding machine

The machine will bend steel sheet up to 16 guage (approx. 1.5mm thick) x 1 metre wide and can produce both box sections, and pans up to 100mm deep (150mm on modified machine).

Once the basic machine has been built it can be adapted in numerous ways to do almost any sheet metal folding job (within the capacity of the machine's strength). Several adaptations are suggested in the optional design section.

Some of the shapes and suggested items which this folding machine can produce are illustrated below.

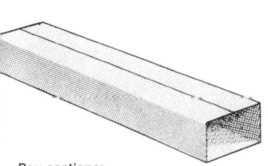

Box sections:
air ducts, chimneys, structural work.

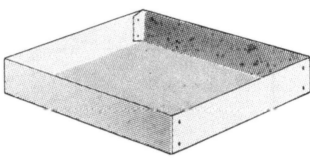

Pans:
boxes, trays, lids, troughs, water/fuel tanks.

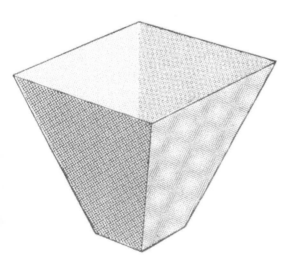

Funnels:
Grain/seed hoppers etc.

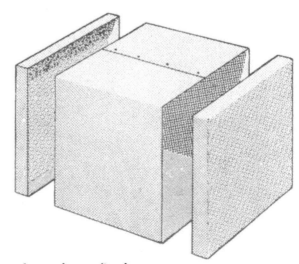

Large boxes/tanks

Description

The machine comprises:

— The base frame assembly, which is suitably fixed down.
— Two clamp assemblies, which act on .....
— ..... the clamping beam, which clamps the sheet metal along the line that requires folding.
— The folding beam which is pivoted at each end. This has a handle which is raised and thus causes the clamped sheet metal to bend. The clamps slide from side to side to adjust to whatever width needed. Several clamping beams can be made to suit the widths of four-sided trays/pans required. This is not necessary for box sections (ducting), or for normal straight folds. In such cases the full width beam can be used.

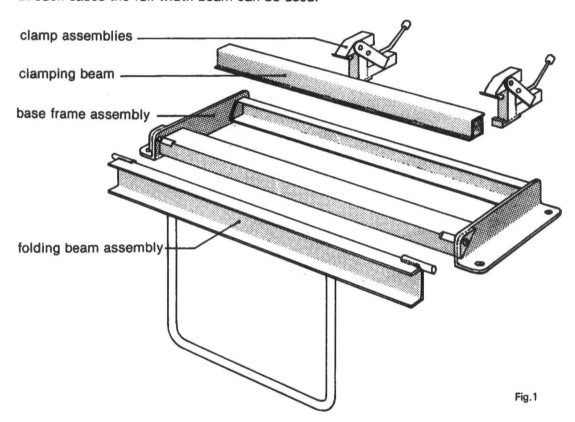

clamp assemblies

clamping beam

base frame assembly

folding beam assembly

Fig.1

7

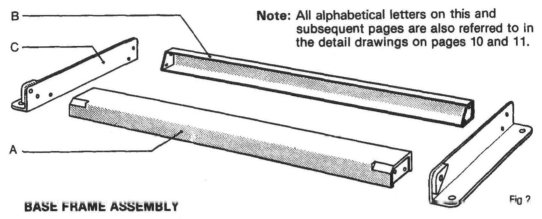

Note: All alphabetical letters on this and subsequent pages are also referred to in the detail drawings on pages 10 and 11.

Fig 2

BASE FRAME ASSEMBLY

This is made up of four separate fabrications: the fixed beam, the clamp slide, and two mounting plates.

A **The fixed beam** has a plate welded in each end, and a piece of angle iron welded underneath to add rigidity. It is also notched at each end to allow for the pivot pins.

B **The clamp slide** serves to take downward pressure as the clamps are tightened, and comprises a piece of angle, strip and two end plates.

C **The mounting plates** are heavy angle iron which serve to fix the machine down, and hold the fixed beam and clamp slide together. They also provide the pivot location for the folding beam.

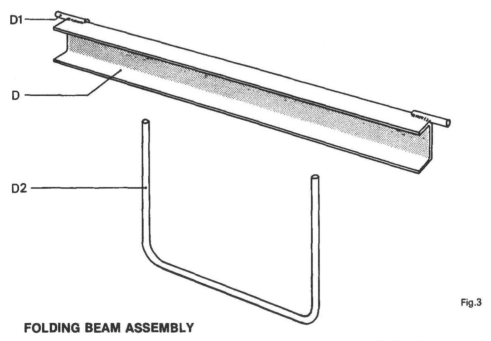

Fig.3

FOLDING BEAM ASSEMBLY

D   **The folding beam** is a plane piece of 100 x 50mm channel. This has recesses cut at each end for the pivot pins which are welded on D1.

D2 **The handle** is of heavy iron pipe welded to the bottom side of the channel.

8

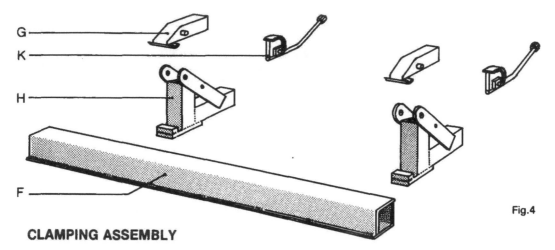

G ——

K ——

H ——

F ——

Fig.4

CLAMPING ASSEMBLY

The clamping beam F can be made in a number of ways, but the simplest is to weld two pieces of angle together. As will be seen from the sectional drawing below they are offset. This is to allow the steel sheet to be bent further than 90° so that it can spring back to a right angle.

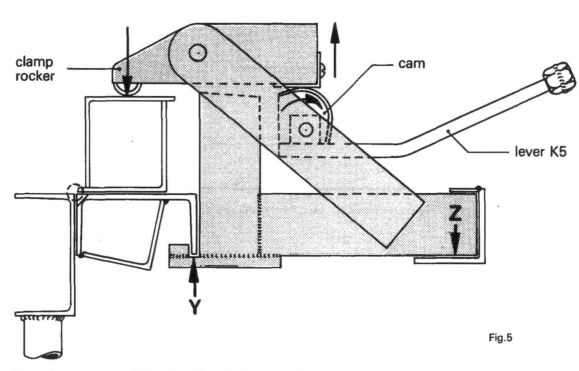

clamp rocker

cam

lever K5

Z

Y

Fig.5

The clamp assemblies G, H and K are designed for quick grip and release action. They are made from 50mm box section (square hollow section, so called). They operate as follows: The lever (K5) is pushed down and turns the cam, causing the clamp rocker to apply pressure to the top of the clamping beam. The result is that point **Y** puts pressure upwards on the back of the fixed beam channel, and point **Z** puts pressure down on the clamp side. The fixed beam channel wants to turn but it is held firm by the side mounting plates.

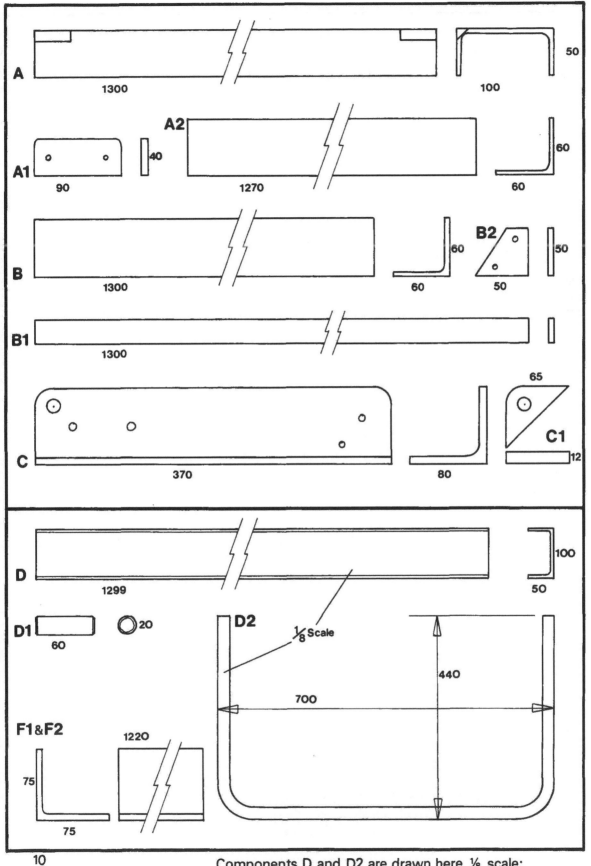

Components D and D2 are drawn here ⅛ scale;
all the other components are ¼ scale.

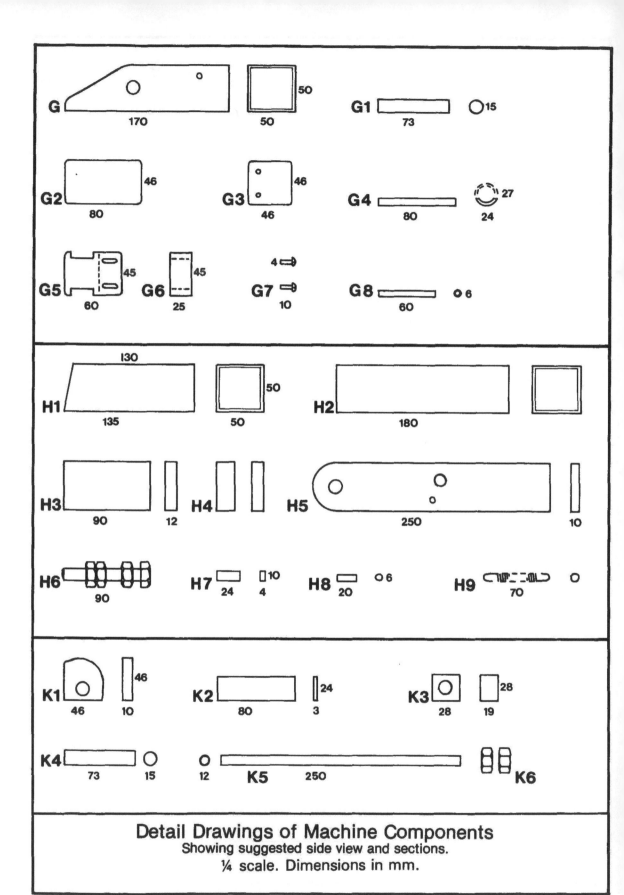

Detail Drawings of Machine Components
Showing suggested side view and sections.
¼ scale. Dimensions in mm.

Construction

BASE FRAME ASSEMBLY — PARTS

Part	Name	Quantity	Dimensions (mm)
A	Fixed beam	1	90 x 40 x 10 x 1300 M.S. channel
A1	Fixed beam end plates	2	90 x 40 x 10 M.S. flat
A2	Fixed beam reinforcing angle	1	60 x 60 x 1270 M.S. angle
B	Clamp slide	1	60 x 60 x 5 x 1300 M.S. angle
B1	Clamp slide cap	1	25 x 5 x 1300 M.S. flat
B2	Clamp slide end plates	2	50 x50 x 5 M.S. flat
C	Mounting plates	2	80 x 80 x 370 M.S. angle
C1	Pivot blocks	2	65 x 65 x 12 M.S. flat

(M.S. = Mild Steel)

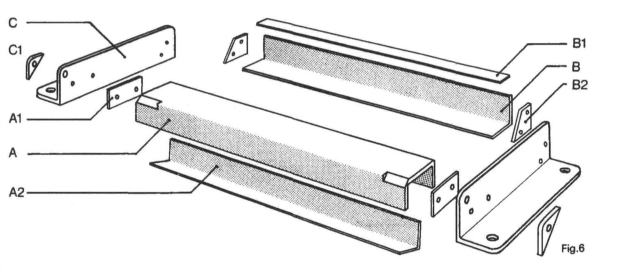

Fig.6

BASE FRAME ASSEMBLY

Cut channel A, angle B and flat B1 to length accurately and file ends square in all planes. Mark out and cut pivot recesses to accommodate the pivot pins. File smooth.

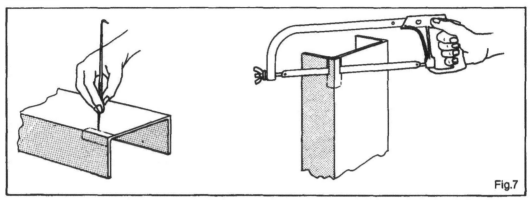

Fig.7

Cut end plates A1 and file to fit inside channel. Clamp in position 3mm short of channel ends and weld in place on inside only. Do not drill and tap yet.

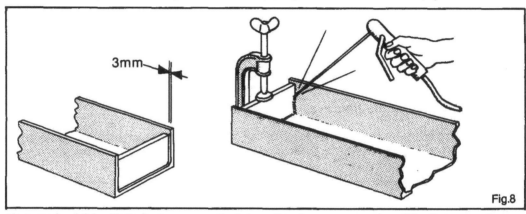

3mm

Fig.8

Cut angle A2 to fit in between end plates. Study cross section (Fig.9) to see how this fits. Position carefully and 'stitch weld' in place. This greatly increases the strength of the Fixed Beam, and prevents it from bending when the machine is used. 'Stitch weld' means put short runs of welds (approx. 25mm) at intervals of about 80mm (in this case).

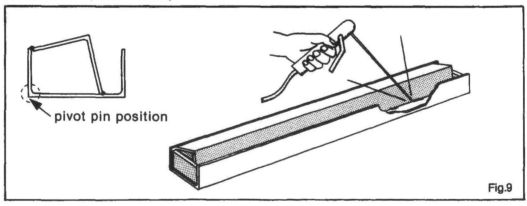

pivot pin position

Fig.9

Mark out and cut clamp slide end plates (B2) and file to fit inside angle B with flat B1 resting on top. Take a piece of 50 x 50mm square hollow section (the same as will be used for the clamp base H1 and H2) to make sure that it will slide along between angle B and flat B1, pack with thin steel and clamp. Position the end plates slightly in from the end of the angle (1mm will do). Clamp, and weld on inside. Stitch weld flat B1 on to angle B. Do not drill and tap end plates yet.

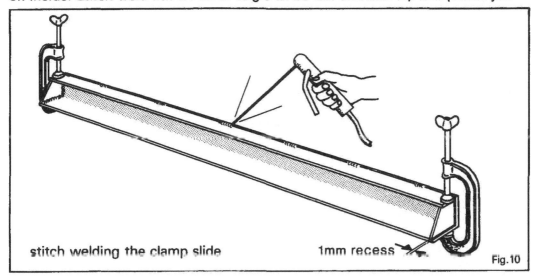

stitch welding the clamp slide   1mm recess   Fig.10

Mark out accurately and cut the mounting plates C. Centre punch and drill all holes with 3mm drill (Fig.11).
Note: Do not enlarge the holes yet.

Mark out pivot blocks C1. Drill hole 3mm, cut out and clean up edges. Clamp to mounting plates and locate hole with piece of 3mm dia. rod. Weld front and top edges only.

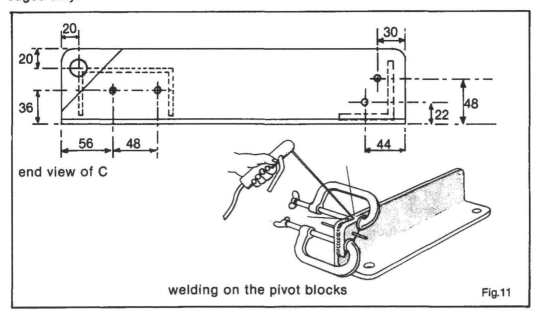

end view of C

welding on the pivot blocks   Fig.11

14

Mark out on the end plates the positions for the ends of the fixed beam, and the clamp slide.

Set up the base frame assembly using packing and clamps, and ensure that:

— all ends are in position;
— the two mounting plates are in the same plane (look along them from one end as indicated) (Fig.12);
— the fixed beam A and clamp slide B are parallel;
— the bottom of the fixed beam A is level with the upper horizontal surface of the clamp side (Fig.11);
— **most importantly**, a 3mm drill inserted in the pivot hole lines up exactly with the corner of the fixed beam (Fig.12). Tap up the fixed beam gently with the hammer until this position is exact, then tighten clamps.

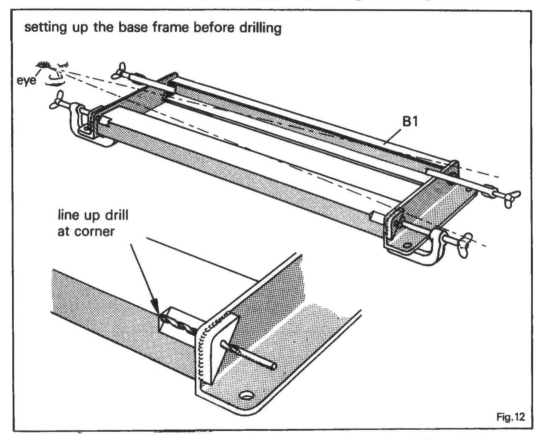

setting up the base frame before drilling

eye

B1

line up drill at corner

Fig.12

Tack weld in place if necessary in order to remove clamps for drilling. Drill holes through into end plates A1 and B2. Break tack welds with chisel and clean off. Remove all clamps. Drill and tap holes in end plates A1 and B2. Drill to size all holes in mounting plates C.

Note: Take care that the pivot hole is accurate and at right angles to the mounting plate. (Sharpen drill first, and use slow speed and lubricant). Check that you have a piece of round bar for the pivots the same size as you are drilling. Check now that the base frame assembly will bolt together properly. File holes out slightly only if necessary. Leave assembled.

Part	Name	Quantity	Dimensions (mm)
D	Folding beam	1	100 x 50 x 1299 M.S. channel
D1	Pivot pins	2	20 dia. x 60 M.S. rod
D2	Folding beam handle	1	25 x 1580 nominal bore pipe M.S.

See diagram on page 7   dia. = diameter

FOLDING BEAM ASSEMBLY

Cut main channel D and file ends square. Check that it fits easily between the mounting plates on the base assembly. Mark out and cut recess for pivot as indicated. It is best to cut on the short side and file the pivot pin slightly as needed.

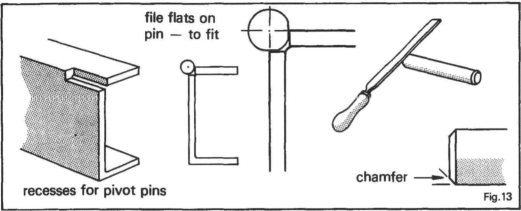

file flats on
pin — to fit

chamfer ──▶

recesses for pivot pins

Fig.13

Cut the two pivot pins D and chamfer ends.

Position pins in holes in pivot blocks, and offer up the folding beam D. File pivot pins until the two tops of the beams are level, and the front faces touch when the folding beam is held in place. Clamp in position and tack pins to beam D.

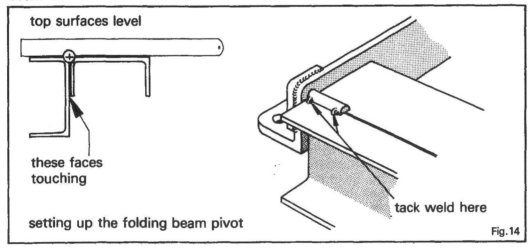

top surfaces level

these faces
touching

setting up the folding beam pivot

tack weld here

Fig.14

Unbolt one end mounting plate, and remove the folding beam. Complete the welds holding the pivot pins. (Make sure these are strong, especially at the outer ends of the folding beam). Refit the folding beam into the base frame and ensure that it will rotate freely, and come to rest right up against the fixed beam. Grind welds and/or fixed beam to accommodate welds as necessary.

Handle — If pipe-bending equipment is available the handle can be made as shown. If not, the handle can be made up either by using some pre-bent tube already available or by welding up elbow pipe fittings. Alternatively, the down tubes can be square section and the cross piece round.

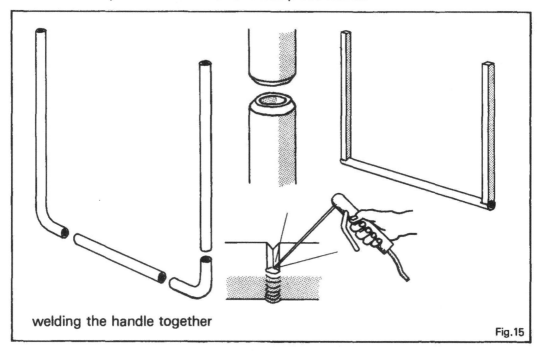

welding the handle together

Fig.15

Locate the handle centrally on the folding beam, and weld in place. Build up a good strong weld as this is a point of stress.

Fig.16

CLAMPING ASSEMBLY —
sub-assemblies

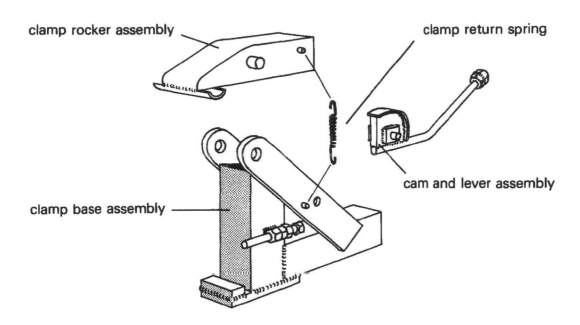

clamp rocker assembly

clamp return spring

clamp base assembly

cam and lever assembly

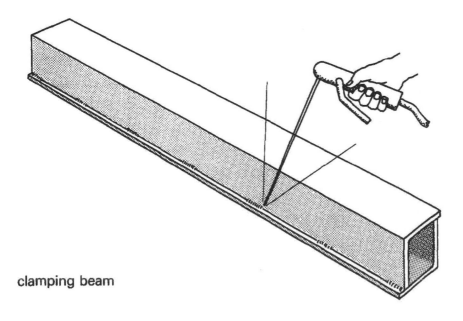

clamping beam

Fig. 17

Part	Name	Quantity	Dimensions (mm)
F1	Clamping beam top half	1	75 x 75 x 1220 M.S. angle
F2	Clamping beam bottom half	1	75 x 75 x 1220 M.S. angle
F3	Stop screw spacers	2	as required

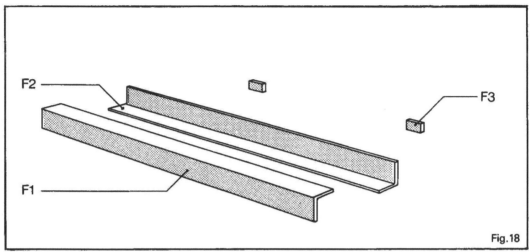

Fig.18

F **The clamping beam** — Cut the two pieces of angle F1 and F2. Position off set and stitch weld as indicated. Put in vice or clamp to any sensible fixed object, and grind or file the leading edge **p**. Check that it is still straight, and correct as required.

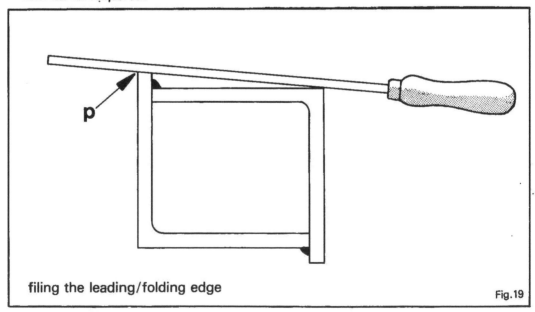

filing the leading/folding edge

Fig.19

CLAMP ROCKER ASSEMBLY — PARTS

Part	Name	Quantity	Dimensions (mm)
G	Rocker body	2	50 x 50 x 170 M.S. box
G1	Rocker pivot	2	15 dia. x 73 M.S. Rod
G2	Rocker top cap	2	80 x 45 x 2 M.S. plate
G3	Rocker end cap	2	46 x 46 x 5 M.S. plate
G4	Clamp foot	2	piece of 27 O.dia. pipe x 80
G5	Cam follower	2	see drawing on page 11
G6	Shim	2	see drawing on page 11
G7	Screws	4	4 dia. U.N.C. x 10
G8	Return spring pin	2	6 dia. x 60 approx M.S. rod

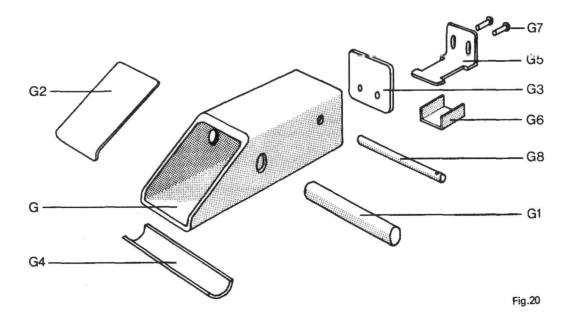

Fig.20

CLAMP ROCKER ASSEMBLIES

Remember to make two of each part whilst marking out and cutting. The following describes the fabrication of one rocker. For dimensions see Fig.21.
Cut the 50 x 50mm square hollow section as shown and drill the holes for the pivot G1. Cut the pivot G1 and position through the rocker, with equal amounts protruding each side. Weld it in place from inside at the front. Cut, bend and file a piece of 2mm plate to fit the front opening and weld in.

Cut a piece of water pipe and file to size shown. Position centrally at tip of rocker and weld front and back.

20

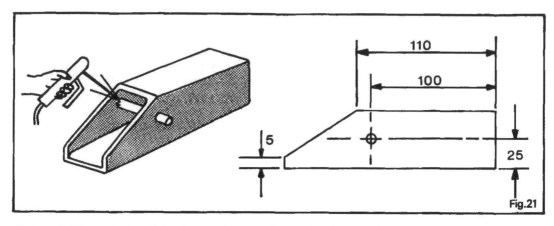

Fig.21

Cut and file a piece of 3 - 4mm plate to fit the back opening, and drill and tap as shown. Fit and weld. (Put screws G7 in whilst welding to avoid getting weld in the threads).

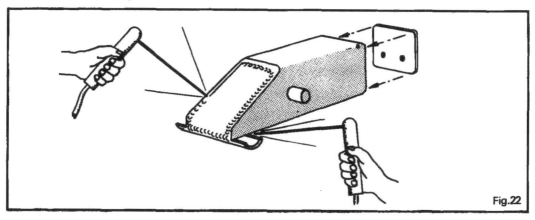

Fig.22

Make up cam follower from 1.5mm steel sheet, and drill and file elongated holes. Cut piece of brass sheet G6 and wrap around G5.

Note: This brass shim can be packed out with more brass or steel shim to increase the clamping pressure. It is also easily replaced if wear occurs.

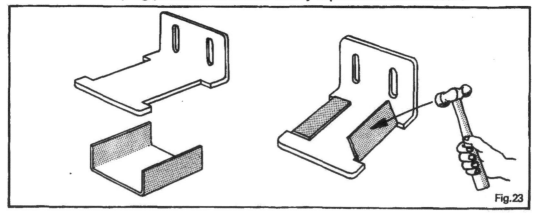

Fig.23

CLAMP BASE ASSEMBLY — PARTS

Part	Name	Quantity	Dimensions (mm)
H1	Clamp base column	2	50 x 50 x 135 M.S. box
H2	Clamp base foot	2	50 x 50 x 180 M.S. box
H3	Clamp base tongue	2	50 x 12 x 90 M.S. flat
H4	Clamp base lip	2	50 x 12 x 18 M.S. flat
H5	Rocker pivot supports	4	50 x 10 x 250 M.S. flat
H6	Clamping beam stop screw	2	12 dia. U.N.C. x 90
H7	Stop screw spacer	2	10 x 5 x 25 M.S. flat
H8	Clamp base return spring pin	2	6 dia. x 20 M.S. rod
H9	Rocker return spring	2	10 dia. x 70 approx

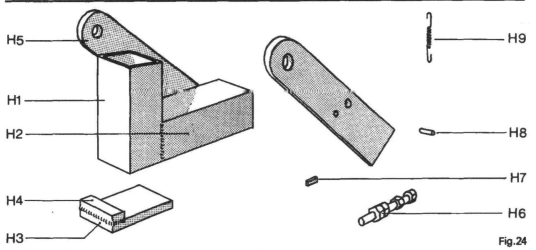

Fig.24

CLAMP BASE ASSEMBLY

Cut H1. Measure the distance between A and B on the main frame, subtract the thickness of H1 (50mm) and 3mm clearance, and cut H2 to this length. Ensure front edge of H2 is a right angle. Clamp and weld. (A woodworker's sash clamp is particularly useful for this).

Fig.25

Cut H3 and H4. Clamp together and weld front and side edges. Clamp H3 to H2. Set the distance of the lip H4 from the column H1 by hooking on to the back edge of the channel A. Shown here upside down.

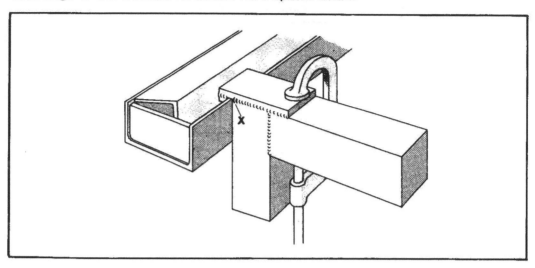

Check that the clamped assembly will slide freely from side to side. Remove assembly from the channel and weld foot on to base both sides, making sure of an extra strong weld at **X**. Mark out accurately, cut and drill pivot supports H5. Clamp one side to the base and position accurately as indicated. Note that the centre of the top hole in H5 must be in line with the front face of H1. Weld in place. DO NOT WELD OTHER PIVOT SUPPORT ON YET.

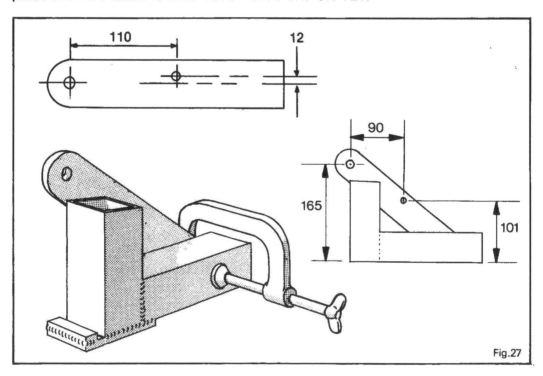

Fig.27

CAM & LEVER ASSEMBLY — PARTS

Part	Name	Quantity	Dimensions (mm)
K1	Cam	2	10 x 45 x 45 M.S. plate
K2	Cam shell	2	25 x 3 x 80 M.S. flat
K3	Cam spacers	4	28 x 28 x 19 M.S. bar
K4	Cam spindle	2	15 dia. x 73 M.S. rod
K5	Cam lever	2	12 dia. x 250 M.S. rod
K6	Cam handle	4	12 threaded nut

Fig.28

CAM ASSEMBLY

Cut out pattern for cam profile. Position pattern on a square corner of a piece of 10mm plate and stick down with tape or clamp on. Centre punch the centre of the cam pivot, and then along the profile of the cam at intervals as shown. Remove pattern and drill hole 3mm and then to size. Cut profile over size and grind almost to line of dots. Finish with a file and check for squareness all round.

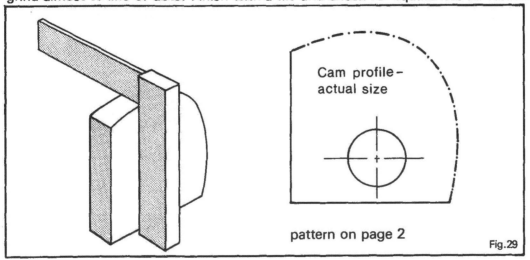

Cam profile-
actual size

pattern on page 2

Fig.29

Cut strip for cam shell K2. Position as shown overlapping each side of the cam equally and parallel with the cam when viewed from the end. Tack weld each side.

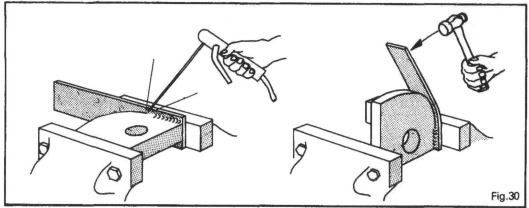

Fig.30

Heat cam shell with a blow torch till red hot, or put in a forge so that only the shell gets red. Clamp in vice and hammer shell round to fit the cam. Clamp tightly round and weld (Fig.30).

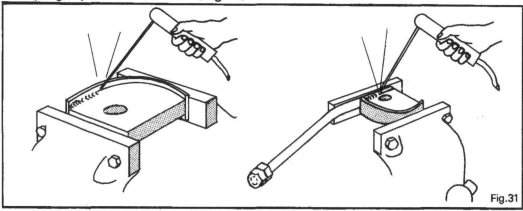

Fig.31

Cut length of rod for lever K5 and find four nuts K6. Bend the lever as shown, and weld the nuts on to the long end. Grind off corners of nuts to make a smooth knob. Clamp the lever on to the cam and weld both sides. Mark out spacers K3 on a bar and drill to size. Then cut off. Cut spindles K4. Assemble spacers and cam on spindles centrally. Weld spacers on to cam.

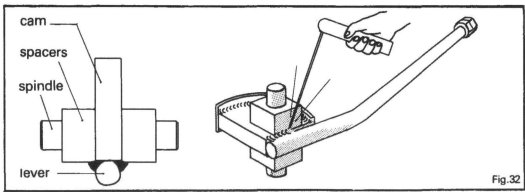

cam

spacers

spindle

lever

Fig.32

ASSEMBLY OF CLAMP

Fit the rocker and the cam on to the pivot support H5 which is already welded to the column. (Grease all pivots and holes first). Fit on other pivot support and clamp ready for welding. Check that the cam and the rocker are free to pivot. If not, insert thin pieces of sheet metal (e.g. piece of tin can) between the pivot support and the clamp column and foot.

When satisfied that the cam and rocker are working freely, (and check that the cam does not foul the column), weld the rocker pivot support H5 onto the column H1 and base foot H2. Also, weld the cam spindle K4 to H5, if necessary to stop it falling out.

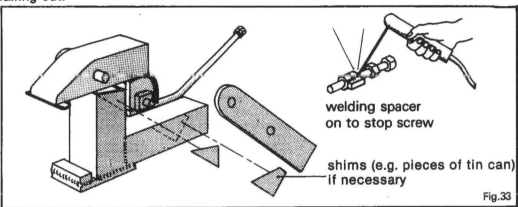

welding spacer
on to stop screw

shims (e.g. pieces of tin can)
if necessary

Fig.33

Stop screw H6 — To complete the clamp assemblies decide on a right hand and a left hand assembly. The left hand one is illustrated (see page 18). Take the bolt H6 and run three nuts down it leaving two of them touching and with the flats lined up. Cut the small spacer H7 and weld it on to the two nuts as shown, top and bottom. Clamp the nuts on to the clamp base column as indicated and weld spacer to the column.
Note: Protect the bolt thread from weld splashes with thin tin wrapped round.

The position of the stop screw is critical. If it is too high you will not be able to get a spanner on the bolt head, and if it is too low you will not be able to fit the clamp assembly on to the fixed beam.

Return spring H9 — Finally cut pins G8 and H8. Cut a small notch about 2mm from one end, to hook the spring on. Pin G8 can be welded flush, on the far side of the rocker. Pin H8 should be made a tight fit and just tapped into its hole in H5, or it can be brazed in. Alternatively, the hole could be drilled and threaded to receive a small bolt with a lock nut. Note that the springs, like the stop screws, need to be on the outside of each clamp. This avoids possible interference with sheet metal being bent between the clamps. Find or adapt a spring to suit and hook on to pins. Grease the cam shell.

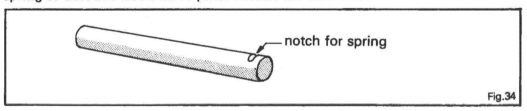

notch for spring

Fig.34

FINAL ASSEMBLY

Remove the clamp slide from the base frame. With a slight twist the clamp assemblies can be hooked on to the back of the fixed beam. The folding beam and the clamp slide can now be fitted. The machine is now ready for use.

26

Operation

Clamp or bolt the base to a suitable bench top. (Ideally a heavy bench or one which is fixed down). Place the clamping beam on top of the fixed beam and under the clamps. Line up the folding edge about 1mm back from the crack between the fixed beam and the folding beam. (This can be adjusted according to the thickness of sheet metal being folded, and the tightness or corner required).

At this point it may be necessary to fit spacers F3 on the back of the clamping beam, where the adjusting screws are to operate. If so, tack weld to clamping beam.

Mark out sheet metal to be folded. Felt tip (spirit ink) pens are ideal for galvanized sheet. Insert the sheet between clamping and fixed beam, until the line is just in front of the folding edge. Push clamp handles down. Raise folding beam handle till required bend is achieved.

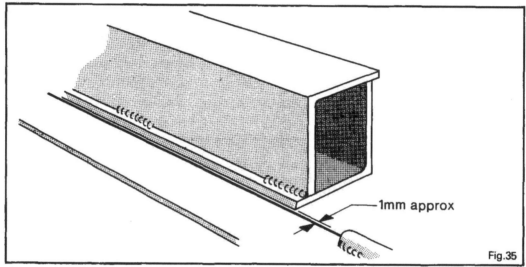

1mm approx

Fig.35

How to fold a pan
A special purpose clamping beam will have to be made for each size of pan you make. (You may already have a suitable one from a previous job.)

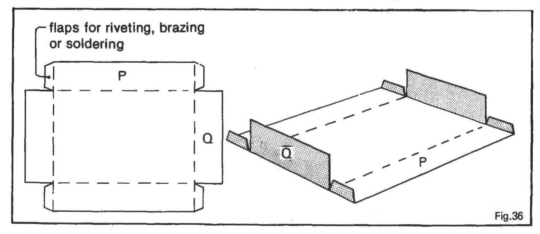

flaps for riveting, brazing or soldering

P

Q

Q

P

Fig.36

Draw the plan of your pan on the sheet metal as in Fig.36, and cut it out. If necessary, make up a clamping beam. It should be 4mm less than the length of the side P (Fig.36).

First bend up the sides Q together with the flaps on the ends of sides P. Before folding sides P, the flaps must be knocked in by an amount equal to the thickness of the steel sheet being used. This can be done on a piece of angle iron screwed to a bench, with a strip of sheet metal tack-welded to the bench to create the required off-set (Fig.37 and 38).

Slide one of the sides P under the specially built clamping beam, and fold up the base. In this process, the sides Q slide alongside the flaps.

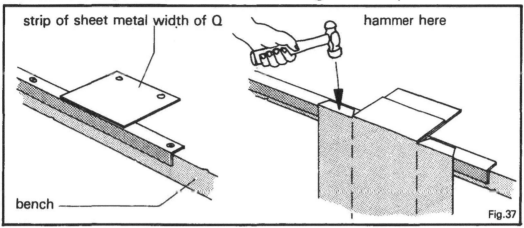

strip of sheet metal width of Q

hammer here

bench

Fig.37

For a number of pans the same size

If many boxes/pans the same size are required, and they need tongues on the corners, the folding machine can be adapted to put the offset on the tongues in one go.

Tack weld strips of metal as indicated, and take care to line them up with the sheet being bent.

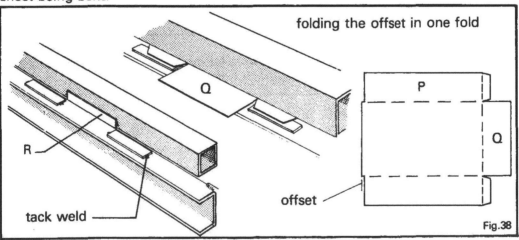

folding the offset in one fold

R

tack weld

offset

P

Q

Fig.38

Slacken off the adjusting screws to line up the front of strip R about 1mm behind the front edge of the fixed beam. Put the base of the box/pan right under the clamping beam and fold up the end Q. The result will be the offset required. Bend P as before.

Optional designs

Folding beam
If it is required to bend return folds as shown, it will be found that the folds cannot be made any closer together than the width of the folding beam (i.e. 50mm).

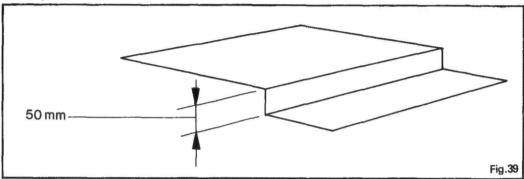

50 mm

Fig.39

In order to do closer return folds, the following alternative folding beam can be made:

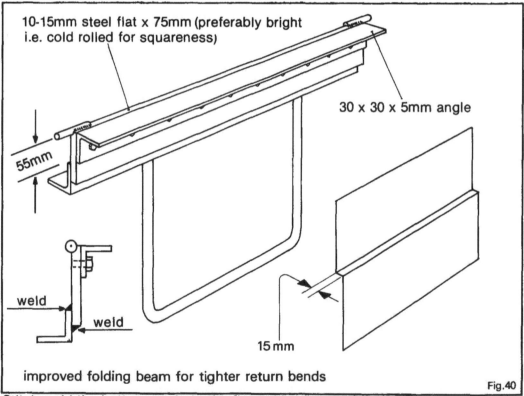

10-15mm steel flat x 75mm (preferably bright i.e. cold rolled for squareness)

30 x 30 x 5mm angle

55mm

weld

weld

15 mm

improved folding beam for tighter return bends

Fig.40

Stitch weld the bottom angle to the flat, taking care to avoid distortion (i.e. weld inside and outside at same place alternately and put more welds on the outside rather than the other way round). This folding beam can be used as normal, but the angle can be removed to do close return bends in light guage metal. This set-up is ideal for car body work, sills etc.

To bend deeper pans
The design detailed in this book will only accommodate pans/trays of depth up to 100mm. To increase this capacity up to 150mm the clamps can be constructed as follows:
— With clamp pivot plates cut from solid 10mm plate (Fig.41).
— With fabrication of 10 x 50mm flat (Fig.42).

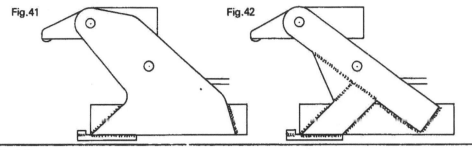

Fig.41   Fig.42

Stand
The stand can be made of 40 x 40 x 4mm angle iron. The important features and approximate dimensions are given in Fig.43, below.

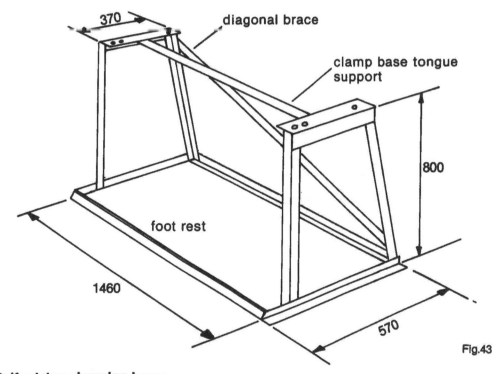

370

diagonal brace

clamp base tongue support

800

foot rest

1460

570

Fig.43

Self raising clamping beam
The clamping beam can be made so that it is lifted automatically when the clamps are released. To achieve this, clamp foot G4 is made instead from 10mm dia round bar; also, loops made from 6 or 8mm dia bar are welded to the clamping beam (Fig.44). The clamp base tongue must be supported on a piece of angle iron or flat bar which runs the entire length of the fixed beam. This can be part of the stand (Fig.43) or can be attached to the fixed beam reinforcing angle.

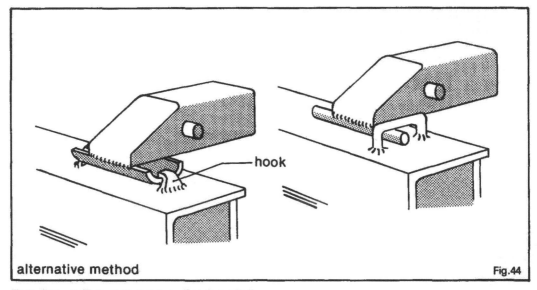

alternative method

Fig.44

Bending radius curves on sheet metal
Special clamping beams can be made up to fold curved corners, as illustrated.

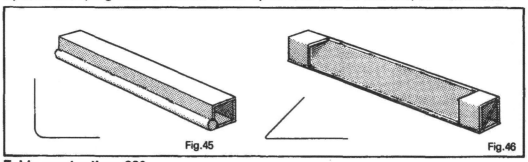

Fig.45

Fig.46

Folds greater than 90°
Special clamping beams can be made to enable folds to be made up to 135°, using a similar fabrication as shown (Fig.46).

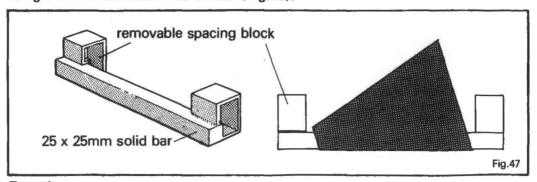

removable spacing block

25 x 25mm solid bar

Fig.47

Funnels
If it is required to fold funnels with a small hole at one end, a clamping beam as shown will handle thin sheet quite well. Remember to make one end removable so the funnel can be slid off.

Check List

(For checks 1 - 6, remove the clamping beam from the machine).

1.   The top surfaces of the fixed beam A and the folding beam D should be straight. Use a straight edge to check this.
2.   Check that the fixed beam reinforcing angle A2 has been installed; it is needed to provide the machine with sufficient strength.
3.   Check that the welding on the pivot pins D1 does not prevent the folding beam from dropping fully when the handle is lowered. Remove any excess weld with a cold chisel.
4.   When the folding beam D is fully down, the top face should be flush with the top of the fixed beam A.
5.   Whilst raising the handle, watch the gap between the fixed beam A and the folding beam D. This gap should not widen to more than 2mm, and should be parallel for the whole length of the beam.
6.   The folding beam front edge should pivot around itself, in line with the centres of the pivot pins. These should be parallel to the folding beam when viewed both from above, and in front of, the folding machine.
7.   View the clamping beam from the end to make sure that there are no sharp bends in it. It should be straight, or deviate only with a uniform curve of not more than 1mm over its entire length. If present, this curve should protrude forwards and/or downwards in the centre, to counteract the upward forces created when the machine is used.
8.   The clamps should slide freely sideways along the frame.
9.   The rocker spindles should rotate with the rockers, and be a good fit in their holes in the pivot supports H5. The rockers should clamp parallel to the clamping beam, work freely and be sprung to return upwards.
10. The adjusting screws and locknuts should turn easily, and the screws should be long enough to locate the beam in its fully forward position.
11. All pivot points and both cams should be oiled.
12. With the clamping beam in position, there should be a gap of 3mm at each end, between the beam and the pivot pins. This allows box-type corners to be folded.
13. Check that the clamp assemblies are left and right handed, with the springs and the stop screws on the outsides.
14. If the clamping beam has been made to be self-raising, a support should have been provided under the clamp base tongues to support them when the clamps are released.

Milton Keynes UK
Ingram Content Group UK Ltd.
UKHW011337070824
1191UKWH00033B/244